## Bb CLARINET

# FILM FAVORITES

### Solos and Band Arrangements
### Correlated with Essential Elements® Band Method

### Arranged by
### MICHAEL SWEENEY, JOHN MOSS and PAUL LAVENDER

Welcome to ESSENTIAL ELEMENTS FILM FAVORITES! The arrangements in this versatile book can be used either in a full concert band setting or as solos for individual instruments. The SOLO pages appear at the beginning of the book, followed by the BAND ARRANGEMENT pages. The supplemental CD recording or PIANO ACCOMPANIMENT book may be used as an accompaniment for solo performance.

ISBN 978-0-634-08691-5

**HAL•LEONARD CORPORATION**
7777 W. BLUEMOUND RD. P.O. BOX 13819 MILWAUKEE, WI 53213

00860143

**From Walt Disney Pictures' TARZAN™**

# YOU'LL BE IN MY HEART

Bb CLARINET
Solo

Words and Music by
**PHIL COLLINS**
Arranged by MICHAEL SWEENEY

00860143

**From the Motion Picture SHREK 2**

# ACCIDENTALLY IN LOVE

Bb CLARINET
Solo

Words and Music by
**ADAM F. DURITZ**
Arranged by MICHAEL SWEENEY

00860143

# Also Sprach Zarathustra

**Bb CLARINET**
Solo

**By RICHARD STRAUSS**
Arranged by MICHAEL SWEENEY

00860143

**From the Paramount Motion Picture MISSION: IMPOSSIBLE**

# MISSION: IMPOSSIBLE THEME

Bb CLARINET
Solo

By LALO SCHIFRIN
Arranged by MICHAEL SWEENEY

From SHREK
# MUSIC FROM SHREK
## (A medley including: Fairytale Opening • Ride The Dragon)

Bb CLARINET
Solo

Music by JOHN POWELL
and HARRY GREGSON-WILLIAMS
Arranged by JOHN MOSS

00860143

**From the TriStar Motion Picture THE MASK OF ZORRO**
# ZORRO'S THEME

B♭ CLARINET
Solo

**Composed by
JAMES HORNER**
Arranged by JOHN MOSS

# PIRATES OF THE CARIBBEAN

## (A medley including: The Medallion Calls • The Black Pearl)

B♭ CLARINET
**Band Arrangement**

Music by KLAUS BADELT
Arranged by MICHAEL SWEENEY

"The Medallion Calls"
**Majestically**

* - new note

**Optional Faster Tempo**

"The Black Pearl"

**From the Paramount and Twentieth Century Fox Motion Picture TITANIC**

# MY HEART WILL GO ON

### (Love Theme From 'Titanic')

B♭ CLARINET
Band Arrangement

Music by JAMES HORNER
Lyric by WILL JENNINGS
Arranged by JOHN MOSS

**From THE MUPPET MOVIE**
# THE RAINBOW CONNECTION

Bb CLARINET
Band Arrangement

**Words and Music by**
**PAUL WILLIAMS and KENNETH L. ASCHER**
Arranged by PAUL LAVENDER

00860143

From **THE LORD OF THE RINGS: THE FELLOWSHIP OF THE RING**
# MAY IT BE

B♭ CLARINET
Band Arrangement

**Words and Music by EITHNE NI BHRAONAIN,
NICKY RYAN and ROMA RYAN**
Arranged by JOHN MOSS

00860143

**From Walt Disney Pictures' TARZAN™**
# YOU'LL BE IN MY HEART

B♭ **CLARINET**
**Band Arrangement**

**Words and Music by**
**PHIL COLLINS**
Arranged by MICHAEL SWEENEY

00860143

**From the Motion Picture SHREK 2**

# ACCIDENTALLY IN LOVE

Bb **CLARINET**
**Band Arrangement**

**Words and Music by**
**ADAM F. DURITZ**
Arranged by MICHAEL SWEENEY

00860143

**Featured in the Motion Picture 2001: A SPACE ODYSSEY**

# ALSO SPRACH ZARATHUSTRA

Bb CLARINET
Band Arrangement

**By RICHARD STRAUSS**
Arranged by MICHAEL SWEENEY

From the Paramount Motion Picture MISSION: IMPOSSIBLE

# MISSION: IMPOSSIBLE THEME

By LALO SCHIFRIN
Arranged by MICHAEL SWEENEY

B♭ CLARINET
Band Arrangement

00860143

# MUSIC FROM SHREK

### (A medley including: Fairytale Opening • Ride The Dragon)

**B♭ CLARINET**
**Band Arrangement**

Music by **JOHN POWELL** and **HARRY GREGSON-WILLIAMS**
Arranged by **JOHN MOSS**

**From the TriStar Motion Picture THE MASK OF ZORRO**

# ZORRO'S THEME

Bᵇ CLARINET
**BAND ARRANGEMENT**

**Composed by JAMES HORNER**
Arranged by JOHN MOSS

# MORE
# FAVORITES FROM
# ESSENTIAL ELEMENTS

These superb collections feature favorite songs that students can play as they progress through their band method books. Each song is arranged to be played by either a full band or by individual soloists, with optional accompaniment on CD.

**Each song appears twice in the book, featuring:**
- Solo instrument version
- Band arrangement for full band or ensembles
- Pop-style accompaniment CD included with conductor's score
- Accompaniment CD available separately
- Piano accompaniment book that is compatible with recorded backgrounds

**Prices:**
- Conductor Books . . . . . . . . . . . . . . . . . . . . . . . . . . $29.99
- Instrument Books . . . . . . . . . . . . . . . . . . . . . . . . . $8.99
- Piano Accompaniment Books . . . . . . . . . . . . . . . . $12.99
- Accompaniment CDs . . . . . . . . . . . . . . . . . . . . . . $12.99

Instrument books for each collection feature separate books for the following: Flute, Oboe, Bassoon, B♭ Clarinet, E♭ Alto Clarinet, B♭ Bass Clarinet, E♭ Alto Saxophone, B♭ Tenor Saxophone, E♭ Baritone Saxophone, B♭ Trumpet, F Horn, Trombone, Baritone B.C., Baritone T.C., Tuba, Percussion, and Keyboard Percussion.

### BROADWAY FAVORITES
*Arranged by Michael Sweeney*
Songs include:
Beauty and the Beast
Tomorrow
Cabaret
Edelweiss
Don't Cry for Me Argentina
Get Me to the Church on Time
I Dreamed a Dream
Go Go Go Joseph
Memory
The Phantom of the Opera
Seventy Six Trombones

### CHRISTMAS FAVORITES
*Arranged by Michael Sweeney*
Songs include:
The Christmas Song
  (Chestnuts Roasting on an Open Fire)
Frosty the Snow Man
A Holly Jolly Christmas
Jingle-Bell Rock
Let It Snow! Let It Snow! Let It Snow!
Rockin' Around the Christmas Tree
Rudolph, the Red-Nosed Reindeer.

### FILM FAVORITES
*Arranged by Michael Sweeney, John Moss and Paul Lavender*
Songs include:
The Black Pearl
Fairytale Opening
Mission: Impossible Theme
My Heart Will Go On
Zorro's Theme
Music from Shrek
May It Be
The Medallion Calls
You'll Be in My Heart
The Rainbow Connection
Accidentally in Love
Also Sprach Zarathustra

### MOVIE FAVORITES
*Arranged by Michael Sweeney*
Includes themes from:
An American Tail
Back to the Future
Chariots of Fire
Apollo 13
E.T.
Forrest Gump
Dances with Wolves
Jurassic Park
The Man from Snowy River
Raiders of the Lost Ark
Star Trek

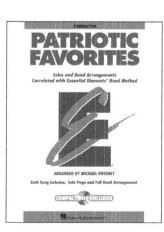

### PATRIOTIC FAVORITES
*Arranged by Michael Sweeney*
Songs include:
America, the Beautiful
Armed Forces Salute
Battle Hymn of the Republic
God Bless America
Hymn to the Fallen
My Country, 'Tis of Thee (America)
The Patriot
The Star Spangled Banner
Stars and Stripes Forever
This Is My Country
Yankee Doodle/Yankee Dookle Boy

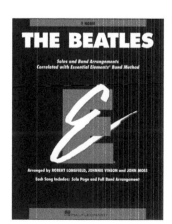

### THE BEATLES
*Arranged by Robert Longfield, Johnnie Vinson and John Moss*
Songs include:
And I Love Her
A Hard Day's Night
Yesterday
Get Back
Lady Madonna
Twist and Shout
Hey Jude
Eleanor Rigby
Ticket to Ride
Here, There and Everywhere
I Want to Hold Your Hand

## HAL•LEONARD®
Visit Hal Leonard Online at **www.halleonard.com**